Projecting Phoebe

Maria Iskander

**Copyright © Maria Iskander
First published 2024**

ISBN: 978--0-9756379-7-5 Paperback

All rights reserved.

Without limiting the rights under copyright reserved above,
no part of this publication may be reproduced, stored in or
introduced into a database and retrieval system or transmitted
in any form or by any means (electronic, mechanical,
photocopying, recording or otherwise) without the prior
written permission of the owner of the copyright.

Published with the assistance of Angel Key Publications
https://angelkey.com.au

Contents

Acknowledgement to Country.................v

Dedication................................. vii

School Season 1

Autumn Season........................... 15

Love Season 21

Winter Season............................ 33

Heavenly Season.......................... 41

Acknowledgement to Country

I would like to acknowledge the Aboriginal and Torress Strait Islanders as the traditional custodians of the land.

I also extend my recognition to the Jagera and the Meanjin peoples to whose lands, I wrote this book on.

Finally, I pay my respects to the Jagera and Turrbal Elders past, present and emerging.

Dedication

I would like to dedicate this book
to Sister Phoebe.

Serving in Alexandria (Egypt), Sister Phoebe
has always guided and mentored me.

And for that, I am forever grateful.

School Season

Education

Education is the passport for tomorrow.
For tomorrow belongs to those
who prepare today.

First Day of School

Your first day of school,
May not be so cool.
But it's the beginning of the countdown;
Where you'll wish you were back at school,
No cap.
For soon you'll grow up,
Realizing that school, wasn't so bad.

Teaching is

Teaching is a work of heart.
You give your smile, energy, and time.
You give people the opportunity to live life.

Students First

Students first.
Sounds great in theory.
But sometimes it causes stress.
Unfeeling.
Students first.
So, I guess, teachers should forget
their wellbeing.
Placing students at the forefront of their minds;
On a pedestal.

Stronger

Every day I been inching to.
Finish the exams that I must do.
The stress is there but I choose to have peace.
You are with me.
Even when I cannot see.

I'm not asking You to make it easier.
But to make me stronger.
Shine Your light on me and my mind.
Help me, guide me to finish on time.

I'm not asking You to make it easier.
But to make me stronger.
This season of daily study is coming.
When will it ever end?
I am slightly afraid, tired and grump.
I can't pretend.

I'm not asking You to make it easier.
But to make me stronger.
I want to do well.
Be noticed.
One of a kind.

I'm not asking You to make it easier.
But to make me stronger- in time.

What we Learn

What we learn, becomes a part of who we are.

School Hurts

I am hurt and confused.
Little tired and bruised.
Told I was doing okay.
Then told I had to go away.

Teaching at school was my dream career.
But now all I have is bitterness and fear.
I am punished for standing up for myself,
Yet encouraged to always contact for help.
Paradoxical.

Students first, I hear this with no end.
No real support for me, a teacher who
needs a friend.
Reports may be filed to keep
paperwork looking great,
But consequences for the student is not at bay.
Keeping appearances.

Students first.
Well, I guess it means that teachers don't
matter this time.
Teachers must be resilient and strong
enough not to cry.
Bottles up.

I have never been so hurt and
confused about life,
Since I entered teaching, as a
profession I worked for;
My whole life.

So, now where do I go?
Where should I begin again?

For teaching sure looked stunning
on the outside,
But on the inside was bitter
Like a deceivingly bitter watermelon.

Perhaps my school,
Where I work for as a busy bee,
Will mention after the matter of facts,
That sit well with me.

Yet, I confess,
I attest,
I contest too.
That my place in keeping my mental health,
Is breaking.
And so, I am truly to blame,
For giving this profession another chance.
Once again.

The Toughest School

Life is the toughest school.
You will never know what class you're in.
Or what exam or test you will have next.
You can't cheat on life.
To be better than the rest.
Even when you try to prepare.
Life will give you questions.
Life will give you choices.
All that will strip your emotions bare.

Why School?

School is hard.
School becomes easier with the tools to

get you through.
Most of the time you'll learn as you do.

School is invaluable.
Schol is a way to learn about practises.
Most of the time you'll find your life axis.

School is Science.
School lets you experiment for a better life.
Most of the time, you'll find it giving you sight.

This Teacher is on Fire (Haiku)

Font must be not 'cute',
Nor small, large, or plain weird too.
Paper will be burned.

Keeping up with School

I am in a generation where I am struggling.
Struggling to keep up with school.
When I don't comply, I look like the fool.

Stressed out like a mouse with no cheese.
Restless like a dog with no owner to please.
Trying to keep up with school.

Materialistic is made as the way to be.
Money matters more than integrity.
This is me- keeping up with school.

I will always love you, School.

Dear School,
Thank you for all the stories I heard.
I never thought I would carry them in my head.
I will always revel the jokes, hugs, and how
you made me smile.
You had my heart.
And you'll always have it.
For it's of no surprise,
On how you taught me wonderful willingness;
The power to try.

Every now and then, it's easy to reminisce
the first time.
First day I stepped into the door.
A door of opportunity for students, fellow
teachers and much more.
You gave me ideas.
Enriched.
With you by my side, in my life.
I was accomplished.

Now, as I embark a new chapter.
Closing this one behind.
I hope you know, dear School,
That I will always love you,
Until the end of my time.

What is a School?

What is school?
Is it a cluster of time,
Which we cherish for life?
Or a moment on top of another moment.
Giving us perpetual strife?

What is school?
Too often I heard it puts your life on track.
But is that really the case when
you find yourself,
Dwelling on the past regrets and mistakes?

What is school?
Sensational for the well off and loud.
Leaving no room for the quiet ones,
Or the lost kids who just want to be found.

What is school?
It's important for both big and small,
Yet leaves a different taste and
experience for all.

Celebrate, Parents!

It's time to celebrate, parents!
School is back and running again.
I am sure your happy your kid's back to school,
For now, you can live your life again.

It's not that you don't like your kids,
I can tell you know them too well.
So much so, that they are an angel in your eyes,
Even if they give the school a new hell.

School Chapter

You cannot start a new school chapter if you
keep re-reading the last one.

Life After School

Like a thief in the dark of the night,
My school years stole years of my life.
Quick.

The feeling was not the same in my
body when I left.
I used to think I would not miss the
order at school.
But now I feel regret.

Life after school is not as great as I
anticipated it to be.
Bill after bill.
Job shift after shift.
Followed by insane hours of study.

I now must remember to eat and go
to the bathroom.
For myself, and my health.

With no bells to remind me where to go.
Life balance doesn't work out as well.
I'm stressed out as if I am in hell.

Life after school.
I never thought I would take it.
Not so well.

Be

Be the leader in a school of fish.

School Times

Flurry of memories and best friends.
Some last forever,
While others no longer happen.
Reminiscing the loyal hearts of gold,
Where you could be brave and bold.

School bells, I should I say 'songs' ran loud.
I remember dancing my way- proud.
Teachers and students were cool all the time.
School life was even better than my
home, sometimes.

School: where 'time flies' takes a
whole new meaning.
School time after time,
Though I'd vehemently deny it,
Was worth living.

Memories

Memories of school cannot be erased.
It's ingrained in my head,
The good, bad, and ugly,
Until the end of my days.

Sleep hits different at School

When in my bed at 6am in the morning,
Hearing the birds chirping, I sleep some more.
Then, for what felt like five minutes rest,
I wake up an hour later,
Rushing to get dressed.

When at school and my day has been so long.
I rest my eyes on my desk.
Then, for what felt like five minutes rest.
I look at my watch and see it's only
been one minute!
The concept of time at school: endless.

Don't Confine

We must not confine the children of today.
With learnings and practises that
are out of date.
We must go with the currents, tides, and waves.
Reminding children that learning is more than
surfing for high grades.

I'm not saying grades aren't important.
They are.
For grades teach us where to improve.
But I'm saying that learning must become,
Greater than just following the rules.

Education currently, needs an update,
Like we have on our phones.
Education must hone on children living,
To make it as a community, not alone.

Education is more than just a 'long marathon'
to finally graduate.
Education must be a gift for everyone:
To feel empowered, acquired, and safe.

School is Magic

Empowering minds, shaping futures – that's the magic of schooling.

Every day in School

Every day in school is a step closer to unlocking limitless potential.

Every day in school, we dream, explore, and grow together.

Every day in school, we try hard to be ourselves, through and through.

Autumn Season

Start over

Don't be afraid to start over
Take the second chance to rebuild
the life you want.
The life you deserve.

Never too late

It's never too late to be, what we
might have been.

Do it!

It is not just about ideas.
It is about making ideas happen.
Do it!

Start Again

Take a deep breath.
Pick yourself up.
Dust off the hate and shame.
And start all over.
Again.

It's Okay

It's okay to make mistakes.
It's okay to be not okay.
It's okay to have hard days.
It's okay to love yourself, every day.
It's okay to not know it all.
It's okay to fall.
It's okay to ask for help and support.
It's okay to be content and bored.

Begin Again

Begin again, and again and again and again.

God's Way

God's way of saying "let's start again"; is in every sunrise and every sunset. So, relax now, my friend.

Butterfly

Just when the caterpillar thought life
was done and over.
While in the cocoon of darkness,
With unrelenting pain,
That caterpillar became a butterfly.
A butterfly: stunning, quick, and ready,
To begin again.

Starting Over

Starting over is not that bad.
For as you restart,
You have a chance.
Another one.
To make things right.
And start over again.

Never

Never feel guilty for the pain you feel.
Never feel like your heart must
be made of steel.

Never feel guilty of not getting it right.
Never feel guilty when you desire to
live: a better life.

Maybe

Maybe it's not always about you fixing people.
Maybe it's about you starting over.
Creating something better.
Maybe it's not always about placing
yourself first.
Maybe it's about realizing your full potential,
despite the hurt.
Maybe it's not always about you saving the day.
Maybe it's just about trying your best, to know
it's okay, not to be okay.

Each Day

Each day is a new day.
Each day is an opportunity for you to take.
Each day is an invitation to be awake.
Each day is not easy.
So be sure to work towards.
The future that you want to create.
A future that is only yours.

Smile

Each day is a new beginning.
So that's why I smile.
And I'll keep smiling like a Cheshire cat:
Little kooky, spooky, and snarky.
For life is too short to be anything,
But the life of one's own party.

Love Season

Love is Pure Living

I used to be so busy for the people I love.
Chasing the next career move,
Stuck in the rat race.
A rut.

I used to be so thirsty for the possessions I
loved in this world.
So much that I'd sacrifice my relationships,
From family to friends.
I thought I was prude.

Now that I am older, slighter wiser.
According to me, not you.
I have learned that love is not getting,
It is giving.
Amen, love is goodness, honour,
Joy and peace.
Love is not of this world,
Love is pure living.

To Love

To love the light, you must learn
to love the dark.

Better

People say it's better to have been loved and
lost than to never be loved. But I call VS.
VS standing for 'very sure'. I call VS that it is
better to love others who don't love you. Yes, it
is better to love those who can never repay you
in love, at all.

Let Everything

Let everything you do.
Have love.
Let everything you say.
Speak love.
Let everything you work on.
Foster love.
Let everything be an avenue to love deeply.
Let everything manifest love, until the
end of your days.

We Come

We come to love not by finding a
perfect person.
A perfect person is like a unicorn
or a hidden gem.
Hard to find or keep.
We come to love by learning to love an
imperfect person.
Whilst, also challenging them to
grow- magnificently.

True Love

True love only exists when it is true.

Love is like a Butterfly

Love is like a butterfly, it goes where it pleases,
and pleases wherever it goes.

You are

You are my favourite person in
Heaven and on Earth.
I love you more than my words can say.
You are my goal and comfort.
I love you deeply- I always will.
You are my number one, until the
end of my days.

In You

In you, I have found the love of my life.
In you, I have found my greatest friend.
In you, I have learned to love truth, not lies.
In you, my broken heart, is now on the mend.

In Love

I'm in love with cities I have never travelled to.
Instagram
I'm in love with people I have never ,
in person, met.
Facebook.

Love

Love didn't meet her at her best. Love met her
at her mess. But didn't leave her in the mess.
No. Love then encouraged her. Inspiring her
to take herself out of the mess. Change. Then
be blessed. Love didn't ask for her perfection.
Love showed her the way out. Giving her the
chance to change. On her own. Love knew she
was lost. And allowed her to be found.

Fairy Tale

Once, in what feels like a millennium,
Right in the middle of a mundane life.
Love gives us a fairy tale,
But not like in the books we read.
Better.
True.
One of a kind.

Loving

You don't just love someone because
their beautiful.
You love someone: deeply, truly, softly.
And by this love,
The person.
Anyone.
Becomes the epitome of beauty.

Those We Love

Those we love don't go away.
They walk beside us each, and every day.
Those we love.
Perhaps unseen or unheard.
Are always missed.
Are always loved.
For those we love,
And have lost.
Stay with us, for us,
Living in us.

Never full

Like the ocean cannot be full of its water.
It daily gives.
Our hearts can not be full of love.
And even if our hearts are.
Our hearts' love will become like a waterfall,
Refreshingly overflowing.

Love's Game

Love is the only game in the world that is NOT
called; on account of the darkness inside us.

Family

Where your life begins, and the love never ends.

Fool

A 'fool in love', is a metaphor
that makes no sense.
For the way I see it.
You are only a fool if you have no love.
As a life with no love,
Is bitter and lonely.
A life with no love,
Is like living on earth, but with no air.

Treat Everyone

Treat everyone like someone you love.
See the difference it makes.
I dare you.

Love Hurts?

Love is not meant to hurt. If love hurts you,
then it's not love.

Love Yourself

Love yourself first, then see everything else
fall into place.

I love you, Egypt!

I love you, Egypt.
You are the country of the golden sand,
A country that follows the Lord's command.
I love you, Egypt.
You are the place tourists and
travellers get to see.
Admiring the glorious pyramids, crumbly sand,
all the way to the Red Sea.

I love you, Egypt.
Recall the 6th of October for me.
It' was the country's great day.
A day that exchanged perilous fights,
For peace and stability.

Egypt, oh Egypt, how I love you too much.
Our history gives me nostalgia,
A feeling of warmth like my mother's bear hug.

I love you, Egypt.
For you were strong to overcome: .
The 2011 Revolution.
Not once backing down.

You were determined to be strong.

With protests and melodies that the people
sang; That attacked your past government,
As well as all its despicable ways.
You remained patient.
Staying on brand.
And as a result, we- your people-
saved the land.

I love you, Egypt.
Sincerely, I don't have the words to say,
How much I adore you.
And wish you the very best.
Each day.
Egypt, you are on the way to maximising
religious peace.
That's why I love you now.
And for eternity.

Love in all you do.

The only way to achieve great things in life, is to have love in all you do.

A Grandmother's Love

A grandmother' love is like an invisible piece of string. Her love connects us to the past, present and future, without us ever noticing.

There is.

Without open and honest communication,
there is no respect.
Without respect, there is no love to be shared.
Without love, there is no reason to continue.
With no continue, there is no more
that can be done.

Love like learning piano.

Love is like learning how to play the piano for
the first time. At the start you practise, practise,
practise. Then rehearse endlessly. By then you
know the rules. But as time goes by, you learn
how to play the piano by heart. True love.
Keeping what is inside of you, pure.

There is.

There is no point- near the end of my days- to
look at what I bought.
There is no point- when I am old, fragile, and
gray- to carry what I built.
I'd rather carry what I shared.
There is no point- when I am buried- to talk
about my significance.
I'd rather be remembered for my love,
A love that surpassed common sense.

Awaken

Awaken self-love, not your ego.

Truly Beautiful Love

There are things more beautiful than a young couple showcasing public displays of affection. Like the couples clasping hands, kissing like fish breathing. Or proclaiming, "I love you; I love you; I love you". Fickle.

The truly beautiful love is from old. A kind of love that doesn't need a boast. Old love precedes social media shares and reposts. It is a kind of love where the man and woman are in sync with one another. Not the internet and people you don't know.

Old love is when you're physically tired. But choose to keep your hearts strong: love and devotion. Old love: truly beautiful love. Is not young and new. Old love is forever. And those who find it, are very few.

The Love in our Family

The love in our family runs fast yet deep. The love in our family, leaves memories; For us to cherish and keep.

Eventually

Eventually, I found myself falling love; Alas, by then, there was no one,
Who could pick me up.

He will never let us go.

What are we doing ourselves?
If we don't have faith or trust.
What are we doing to ourselves?
If we chase our temporal lusts?
For the souls of mankind anywhere.
He is our perfect guide and strength.
One and Only, no one can compare.

Truly and forever, may we know.
How much he loves us.
He will never let us go.

She

She speaks loud and clear.
She smiles with no ounce of fear.
She is always there- even not physically.
Like a glue, she holds tight this family.
She's a very successful mum.
Overcomer of struggles - under the sun.

Achieving the impossible.
She has kept us safe, holy, and humble.
A light to keep us from going blind.
She is a graceful power- one of a kind.
Comforter for our silent sadness, A rock in the loud madness.

She cares for us- way overtime.
Her love for us goes the extra mile.
She is a good mother- trustworthy and kind.
She is a beacon of hope in the worst of times.

She is a cheerleader in our times of stress.
She always gives feelings of peace and rest.
She is a mother, like you and me.
She is a mother here for you- eternally.

To Love Yourself

Your greatest responsibility in your short but sweet life is to love yourself. With no bounds or conditions. To love yourself with all your power and might.

Winter Season

We are all Human

Where do we catch our breath? Where can
we draw the line?
Another terror has taken place.
Once again taking an innocent life.

It may not be Christians,
It may not be people you knew.
Yet, the death still stings through.

Muslims and Coptic Christians in Egypt.
Both Human, bleeding the same.
With desire for love and mercy.
Instead of bloodshed and pain.

We are all fallen and broken, in some
way or another.
Although it's never easy, may we
sticky by each other.
No difference in skin.
Religion.
Culture.
Or belief.
Will ever justify these spiteful killings.

People

People that are evil like days on end. Are
the people who will fail you. There is no
doubt about it.

People that will hurt you. Are the people you
can live life without. So, stop obsessing on why
they behaved. And start living your life today.

People will burn you. Figuratively more than literal. So be sure to not burn yourself, when you wait for change in people.

Own It

When the sadness comes knocking at your pre-frontal cortex door, be sure to acknowledge it, once more.

Then, after sadness has gotten tired- and finally leaves, joy will cruise in your Hypothalamus.
Giving you a pleasant win:
Mi 'amor.

She cried.

Life getting her overboard.
Feeling like a piece of dust
Without a cause.
More people mistaking her for a rock-like steel,
Little did they know that she wanted to heal.
Fellow friends all just assumed.
That she was 'over it'.
It's a suicide.
Not a lifelong gloom.
The world and its people have broken her,
Once and for all.
For she was not made of steel.
She cried.
She needed someone to call.
She needed to heal.

Red, White, Green

Red, white, green
What does it mean?
Christmas colours all over the place
Or Israel and Palestine's festering, insane
and terrible fate?

Red, white, green
What do you see?
A time for beauty from Christmas
fashion or decor
Rather than reminding -yourself- on the people
suffocating from war.

Red, white, green
What do you feel?
Gratitude, subliminal messages, and rest
While other people- 'not your problem'- die
from hunger and distress.

Red, white, green
Three colours that mean a lot,
For many it's merely symbolic of
Christmas fun and cheer.
When for others- gone and present- the colours
are an expression- suppression, spite, and fear.

You Stabbed Me

You stabbed me a thousand times.
You stabbed me.
Then acted as if you were the one bleeding.

Addiction

Tablets scattered on the table and the floor.
I think I've become addicted to a
temporary cure.

Sooner before I know it- trapped.
Lingering in this destructive path.

So many lies keep feeding my soul.
Deceiving lies that chain my will to call,
To call a friend, parent, any sane
person- to help.
Instead, I choose to keep snug with a
minuscule tablet.
Oh well.

Truth be told- miserable, lonely, and small- I
have lost my sense of self. I don't know who I
am anymore.

I don't know.
I never will.
Nor can anyone have the right words to say.
How I can turn around one day.

No longer

No longer want to keep playing to your
evil schemes. No longer want to partake in
your fickle dreams. No longer will I fall for
your sugar-coated explanations of what is
completely bad. You have made me a fool. I
can't believe I allowed you to. Now, get with
it. We are done. No longer do I want to see
you- or anyone.

You vs Me

You say you want be friends
and miss me dearly.
Then I get your snaps of you at a party, and it points to me clearly,
That your words are empty and you're playing games.
I need honesty and so don't think that it's me being anti-social or lame.
If I decline to come to your places, know that I can't bother anymore,
With you, or your lies that keep making, My fragile heart sore.

My eyes are finally open.
You know the saying: I'm blind and now I see.
Because finally, I understand your scheme.
You try and make me the problem- always.
Throwing lies back and forth with no shame.

Three "I"

There may be no "I" in team. But there are three "I"s
in "narcissist".

Narcissistic Personality Disorder

Narcissistic personality disorder is the only mental condition where the patient is left alone, but everyone else needs treatment.

Narcissistic People

Narcissistic people have an inflated sense
of self- worth.
A delusion of self-importance.
One could say an extreme
preoccupation with no one;
But with one's self.

Closure, with a Narcissist

You will never be given closure to a relationship
with a narcissist.
Better for you to know earlier than to
foolishly expect it.

With time, I have learned that narcissists are
great in the power play.
Keeping you hanging on,
While hoping they will change.

Truth be told.
A narcissist does not change for the better.
They move on.
Returning worse than before.

Narcissists intentionally leave you guessing,
On eggshells, wherever you may go.

A narcissist will never apologize.
For they know they hurt you.
They don't care.

Yes, it's hard to swallow,
But truth be told,
The only closure you can count on,

Will be from yourself.
So, close the door on the narcissist,
Start your life without them,
And never look back.

Heavenly Season

We are His

For if we died ,
With Him,
We'll also live.

For if we endured,
We'll also reign.

For if we are faithless,
He remains faithful.

He is God,
We are His.

One and Only God

Again, Jesus spoke to them, saying, 'I am the
light of the world.
Whoever follows Me will never
walk in darkness.

Then the Pharisees said to him, 'You are
testifying on your own behalf.
Your testimony is not valid to harness':
Jesus answered so humbly and said,
'Even if I testify on my own behalf,
My testimony is valid because I know
where I am kept.
But you do not know where I am coming from
or where I am going.
Instead, you judge by human standards; yet
I judge no one'.

As He spoke these words while he was teaching
in the temple's treasury,

No one dared to arrested him, for fear of an
uproar of people- anarchy.

Clearly, Jesus spoke of Himself as the truth.
Confident that he embodied God's presence.
Indeed, He was not shaken by Pharisees' cries
of "False witness!!"

From this we can learn that Christian faith is
much more than doctrine.
It is a person.
Through this person- Jesus Christ:
We can cherish the mystery of the Holy Trinity,
Divine with Humanity
The One and Only God.

Seek First

Seek first to understand and employ empathy
for what strangers go through.
Seek first to respect and intrinsically appreciate
what others do for you.
Seek first to change and be accountable
of every action.
Seek first to be the start of a 'love'
chain reaction.
Seek first to love yourself when you
feel unlovable.
Seek first to nourish your faith, even when its'
uncomfortable.
Seek first to intrigue others to grow in
joy and grace.
Seek first to leave your light, in
every single place.

Struggling Strong

In the beginning, we- mankind, were created
with a spiritual instinct.
An instinct to show mercy, give to the poor,
issue prayer and fasting.

Yet as the obstacles of life come in
the way at times.
We find ourselves struggling to keep
our spirits alive.
The way of effective and constant prayer, as our
Lord Jesus would say.
Is to struggle strong and be encouraged
to always pray.

Yet often we fall in praying because we lost
heart too quick,
Or become discouraged to no longer pray-
as we overthink.

Prayer is hard work and requires us to
struggle strong.
It is not approached lightly or keep count of
someone's wrong.
To pray with a pure heart, is to
forgive and understand:
That Lord Jesus is God, and so we must love
our fellow man.

Do you recall the parable about the ungodly
judge and the woman who sent a request?
After the woman's persistence to bother him,
that ungodly judge finally listened.

Jesus did not give us this parable to say that God is reluctant to help us.
But to teach us to not lose heart in prayer, and to put in God our trust.
Our God is never reluctant to answer the desires of our hearts.

Our God is a God of justice and mercy and restores our broken pasts.
Our God gives us special grace to struggle strong and not lose heart.
Our God remains compassionate right from the start.

To the some who trusted in themselves that they were virtuous,
Of those whose vain pride, led them to lose all real connection.
We can learn from those that if we credit ourselves a supposed great, spiritual way.

Then, it will become an easy thing to despise another each day.
Thus, in place of vain credits and judgement of another's nature and limits.
We must pray always, living with the memory of God's forgiveness.

Indeed, this is the crux of us building character and struggling strong.
It is a procession of being kind , gracious, and not scorekeeping of others doing wrong.

Filled

As in the past, He still says to us to give the
multitude something to eat.
A wonderful provision made for the famishing
the weak, broken, downtrodden and beat.

It is a figure of the Holy Gospel we read.
But people do not read as they did before.
So, we must manifest the Holy Gospel to all.

Sounds simple, and yet deeply
important and difficult.
How can we make people feel filled?
As those disciples who received the loaves and
fish from Christ's hand.
May we able to carry the little and make
an iconic plan.

As those disciples were a figure of all faithful
teachers back in the day.
May we able to graciously fill the destitute and
the misplaced.

Perfecting Purity

No one after lighting a lamp put it away,
but on a stand.
Hence, no one that enters may see the
light put away.

Our eye is the lamp of our body-
divinely planned.
So, when our eye is good, then our whole
body cannot decay.

The decay in our body , comes from
darkness and sin.

Therefore, to have our bodies full of light is a
wonderful thing.
As Jesus said, something greater than Solomon
and Jonah is here.
Alluding to the wisdom of Jesus, exceeding
human wisdom to sphere.

Indeed, the Resurrection of Jesus, remains
greater than any spectacular human rescue and
resuscitation.
The questions Jesus addresses to us are:
Do we see His Resurrection for what He is –
magnificent and powerful?

Do we see how He became the light and joy
keeping our cups full?

He talked about seeing- and about two lamps.
One for our vain fix.
One for serving God and our fellow man.

Let's take this to mean that the lamp we choose:
Has power to make us spiritually win or lose.
There are many bright things in the
world currently.
Things that keep us from seeing the true
light of Christ.

So, may we be careful and take this
imperative seriously.
Giving Him the glory and honour through our
love and sacrifice.

Indeed, may the Lord, open the eyes of
our hearts today.
Filling us with His presence as we seek His
light each day.
Also, may our eyes be good and strong to put
the devil at bay.
Thus, perfecting purity- making us holy and
unashamed.

Who is That?

Nothing, in short, can explain.
The finger of God in our place.
The same hand which sent manna from Heaven.
Was the same hand that made five
loaves and two fish.

The same hand that made five
loaves and two fish,
The same hand that fed five thousand,
Was the same hand who taught us
how to forgive.
The miracle before us, is one of many proofs.
Proving that with Christ nothing is impossible.
His provision is a gift.

He loves us even in times when we're aloof.
The Saviour of sinners is always Almighty.
He calls those things not as though they were.
He created light out of the darkness.
Brining joy out of weeping and sorrow.

Who is that who wallows in despair from
the corruption?
Of our human nature and current deception.

Who is that who makes our heart
blocked- concrete?
Like those unknowing, the power
of the Almighty.

Who is that who asks such questions?
With hopes to find answers:

Can these dry bones live?
Or can any man or woman be saved?
Can any child, or friend of ours forgive?
Or can anyone live for Him, unashamed?

I, it is me, who asks such questions amiss.
I, it is me, who falls in the dark abyss.

Indeed, poor, and despicable, was my story,

Before the crucified Saviour came.
Foolish and lost, I was a worry.
Before the power of God gave me faith.

So now, I have questions for another thing.
On what emblem of Christ is striking.
I see in as a mirror of some sort.
As the most important truths of
Christianity, taught.
As Christ always supplies our spiritual needs.
Let's be sure to thank Him, incessantly.

He lives in Heaven, up away.
Waiting for us to travel there one day.

Who is that gracious Teacher?
Who has compassion on the multitudes.
Who is that great storyteller?

Who left us parables and a Holy Gospel.

Is it Jesus Christ, our God.
As well as the Holy Spirit in form of a dove.
Three in One, One in Three.
Is our God, who unconditionally gave us love.

He is every full of pity,
Ever kind.
He is ever ready to show mercy:
Even to the spiritually blind.

Who was that multitude which surrounded
our Lord again?
It was I, the poor, helpless and destitute.
A lowly human unsure what to do.

Who is that a bright constant?
Who not even once, has altered on anybody.
Is it Jesus our Father and Almighty.
Who chose to cherish and love us- humanity.

What do you Value?

People value being true to themselves.
And some value impressing others.
People value doing good for a social fame.
And some value doing good for
humanity's sake.
People value being kind to others, and true.
And some value never spending money on you.
People value conforming to the lies.
And some value living in the truth- all the time.

Targeted Time

In the Beginning, He made the world
out of nothing,
Caused animals, light, plants, and food to exist.
Blessings which before, had not existed.
The Timeless became timebound when
he was incarnate.
He used the same power which
created the world,
And the line of humanity.
With targeted time, two fish and five loaves.

He fed over five thousand people.
Without expecting anything in return.
With targeted time, there's no
room for mistake,
About the reality of His power and might,
Sufficient for our daily needs- day and night.

Cleaving to Good

You are constant followers,
Christian ministers to all.
Taught by Him.

Cleaving lessons, big and small.
Out was a loss.
To know namely, the parables.

Parables on watching servants.
Begging their Master satisfy.
Parables on watching servants,
Who hereafter waited for the Christ.

You knew indeed these Parables.

You knew who it was to address.
Addressing to all the disciples,
Containing instructions for them to covet.

His parables contained instructions
for them to covet.
His parables contained instructions.
Which Peter thought might be peculiar.

Parables designed for the big twelve,
Parables concerned with faithfulness sooner.
Entrusted with the care and the Word,
You remain to be great role models.

On what it takes to have character and conduct,
And make sense of such these words.
You are stewards to whom He committed with:
The care of His family- the church.
In his temporal absence.

I am who I am,
But I too want to cleave the good:
Reject evil.
Love and give.
Be perfect.

Seek the Kingdom.
Pray, submit,
And care for the greater good.

I want to be a steward,
To whom the Lord commits.
Why certainly, I plan to be both wise.
As much as prudent inside.
I'm under Your care.
I'm trusting Your provision.

Never will I remit my care,
Following Your path is my mission.
As the disciples saw the unspeakable,
Followed by the importance of living simply.

I too, want to live happy and faithful,
Patiently honouring my gracious Lord.
You promised to commit management,
Trust in which a servant shows merit:

In prudence, faithfulness, and diligence,
A type of trifecta to compare with.

I, too, want to cleave the good:
Not only in consciousness,
Of doing His duty well.
A patient continuance.

Pas' d' air (No Air Without Jesus)

I lay down and feel unrest.
Heart out and put to the test.
Stuck in here, deep down inside.
I am trying to stay positive all the time.
Can't complain, but I still bleed.
Missing your presence with me.

I miss Your aroma on my clothes.
I miss You seeing my weird toes.
I miss Your taste in my mouth.
I miss You from the inside out.

Shame is on me for not visiting enough.
Shame is on me for not taking Your love.
I was not ready- never was.

So, I would always delay. The fear inside me,
took a hold, and so I kept running away.

Now, I'd do anything to see You,
To be cosy at Your place again.
I'd do anything to talk to You,
To have Your touch again.

The cruel irony of this very day,
is how a world was brought to its' knees, From
a virus that carried away.
As people died from this virus;
Due to a lack of air,
Your absence from me,
Is totally not fair.

My longing for you - even after Your gone,
Proves that I have been a fool all along.
I am a fool, I am a fool,
Indeed, I am a fool;
For ever thinking I could live,
Without You.

Sollie

These tears on my pillow,
Are too many,
Sollie's loss on Earth makes me hollow.
But I still look forward to tomorrow.

Sollie is like a shadow in the moonlight,
A whisper of the Seven seas.
Sollie is like the echoes of a melody,
Just beyond my reach.

In the shadow of this sorrow,
Way past the whisper of goodbye.
Sollie's love shines through eternity,
In my heartbeat and twinkle of an eye.

Sollie, I will always remember your
infectious smile,
A sense of humour that would make people cry.
Sollie, you had a caring heart- a heart
made of gold.
Sollie, you lived life with valour and were bold.

I and countless others were made better
by Sollie. He left a mark of kindness,
through and through.

So, let me thank you Sollie,
For being in my lifetime.
I- as countless others- will always love
you Immensely,
Until the end of our time.

Indeed, this is not the end of
connection with Sollie,
But only the beginning.
For I and countless others, will one day
journey up there.
Seeing you in Heaven.

Letter from Sollie

Dearest,
Perhaps, you are still not ready yet.
Perhaps, you thought of things:
You wish you had done or said.

So here are some things I'd like to say.
But first, I want to let you know that I am okay.
I am in Heaven, dwelling with God above.
A place with no sadness or pain, just
praise and love.

I am sorry for when you feel overwhelmed as I
am out of sight.
But I promise to be with you: morning,
noon, and night.

On that day I had to leave, I went through.
St Barbara took me to God, who hugged and
welcomed me too.

They told me: 'It's good to have you, we missed
you while you were gone'.
'As for your dearest, they'll be here later on'.

Next, God gave me a 'to do list' of things He
wished me to do.
And foremost on this list, was to watch
and care for you.
So, whenever you struggle to sleep at night.
Just know that I am with you, right by your side.

When you remember of my life on Earth, all
those epic years.

I understand that you're only human and may
be bound to tears.

So, don't be afraid to cry, as it'll relieve the pain.
Afterall, there would be no flowers or trees
without any rain.
There are many rocky roads ahead of you and
many more hills to climb.
But together we can do it by taking
one day at a time.

It was always my intention, and I hope it
will be yours too:
That you live in this world, but not
conform to its woos.
If you can help someone everyday, in
their sorrow or pain;
Then you can say to God each night: 'My day
was not in vain'.

Now, as I am contented with my life
being worthwhile.
I'm forever grateful that I made you smile.

When you walk or drive to church, work or the
like, and got me on your mind.
Know that I am walking in your footsteps, only
half a step behind.
And when it is time for you to go, from the
body and be free.
Just remember, my love, that you're coming
to God and me.

www.ingramcontent.com/pod-product-compliance
Lightning Source LLC
Chambersburg PA
CBHW042226160426
42811CB00117B/1019